Twice Under the Sun

Anna Glazova

Twice Under the Sun

Translated by Anna Khasin

Shearsman Books
Exeter

First published in the United Kingdom in 2008 by
Shearsman Books Ltd
58 Velwell Road
Exeter EX4 4LD

ISBN 978-1-905700-92-9
First Edition

Copyright © Anna Glazova, 2008
Translations copyright © Anna Khasin, 2008
Introduction copyright © Geoffrey Squires, 2008

The right of Anna Glazova to be identified as the author of this work has been asserted by her in accordance with the Copyrights, Designs and Patents Act of 1988. The right of Anna Khasin to be identified as the translator of this work has likewise been asserted by her. All rights reserved.

Contents

Preface by Geoffrey Squires   7

Twice Under the Sun   15

Preface

The initial thing that strikes one about this work is its consistency. There is no wavering, searching for a register: from the very first poem we are thrown into a type of writing which is sustained, with very little deviation or let up, until the last: something that is immediately identifiable and which quickly becomes so familiar as to seem inevitable, even natural. There are of course some variations in the substance and form of the poems, reflecting no doubt changes over the period of seven years' work represented here, but in the end it is the unity and integrity of the whole that leaves the lasting impression.

That consistency must also have something to do with the translation. I have seen some other translations of Glazova's work which actually seemed to me more fluent and easier to read, but I suspect that Anna Khasin has preserved a necessary obduracy and jaggedness in the writing. These are mainly short poems, consisting of short lines, often with syntactic breaks within them; so that when occasionally one does come across a long, fluid line, the effect is all the more lapidary:

like those waves were breaking in you not in the sea you swam
(p.73)

So what kind of consistency is it? Loosely, one might call it a unity of style, except that this implies some kind of space between intention and execution, a matter of writerly choices, whereas here it seems to pertain to the very constitution of the poems. It is hard to imagine them otherwise. The very dislocations within them are part of them, part of what they 'say'; one has the sense that they necessarily came out this way. They are also very dense, compressed: miss a line and you've had it.

So what about 'voice'? In some of the poems, certainly, there is the expression of a self, the conventional subject and source of the personal lyric. That emerges typically as a sudden, abrupt comment or question so are we alive (p.17)

right, let's go (p.49)

what, what time is it, now? (p.60)

There is also sometimes an explicit or palpable 'you', and some of the poems imply dialogue, relationships of tenderness, anger, closeness, dismay, complexity:

the way I hear you, you hear.
lay fingers on my mouth
i will
lay fingers on your fingers (p.40)

blue.
like the sky like the sea like the sound wave
i am silent with, i have agreed not to sing
as we talk (p.39)

hiding hands in the glove of each other (p.27)

listen, all right, lie, lie, but at least with feeling (p.69)

The personal pronoun is complicated in some cases by compounds which apparently come more easily to Russian than to English: she-i, he-i, it-her, not-you. This points to fissures in identity, and while there a pervasive sense of self in the work, unlike in much post-modernist writing where the very idea of the agentic subject has dissolved into language itself, it is a complex, intermittent, transient sense, which can disappear the very moment it materializes: 'to erase yourself after yourself' (p.21). The personal voice typically functions as intrusion or interpolation in something else:

me, I'm kind of not here. dust. (p.69)

The texture of the writing is so close and compressed that it is difficult if not impossible to separate out the conventional elements of self, object, situation; what we have is a cognitive process, a highly distinctive consciousness, both embodied and disembodied, which cuts across the usual distinctions and categories, and where one word or image often leads directly on to another, without reference to what preceded it, in a kind of weirdly logical, sometimes dreamlike (or nightmarish) progression. This consciousness is grounded in a strong physical, material and organic sense of the world (which is even more evident in the prose pieces at the end of the book): there are frequent references to the body (hands, eyes, throat, skin, pores) to food and the vegetable (oil, honey, apples, figs, berries, pods) to rocks, metals, fish, insects, animals or beasts. Sometimes these occur as blank, random, factual lists:

from it fall
wool, feather, salt
ash, nitre. (p.66)

At other times, there is a surreal mixing of forms:

a fish standing in a flood changes,
grows hooves in the fins maybe
or maybe its body abates (p.65)

Or a sensuous blending of elements, though the gaps and disjunctions are as important as the substances:

heavy oil unglowing honey
you tell me in my skin and mouth: "the nape" and the fingers
    are in the hair

i hold the shy bunch
berries maybe or silent beasts

if they fall, will they break?—silence (p.30)

There is also frequently a sense of minute detail, as if the level of magnification had been turned sharply up:

terrible to hold to the light
in the index and thumb
of a skinned grape
a small heart.

when suspended from every finger
swings a world. (p.18)

This physical or material sense of the world is counterbalanced by something which I can only call an abstract imagination, a capacity to express what is not:

lamplight falls into no hand (p.62)

you measure air with your back (p.48)

It is this alliance of sensuous and abstract, present and absent that makes these poems so distinctive, giving an almost tactile sense of void, of what is not. Sometimes the very process of perception is thrown into doubt: 'the black sea the blue sea'; 'without a mirror with one' (p.28). One can take nothing for granted, and in this perhaps one can see a shadow of Heidegger's *Unheimlichkeit*, literally not-at-homeness. There is an alternating sense of location and dis-location, familiarity and strangeness, ease and unease. There is also a recurring preoccupation with the internal, with being inside, containment of various kinds:

we have bent the wall so
that all doors are outside
and inside is the sea (p.37)

if the inside of the fog is soft
let's fall there (p.63)

which blurs the boundary between the inner and outer worlds.
And the very categories of perception are at issue:

the eye which I remember by ear (p.67)

All through there is the effort to articulate, the over-riding need to speak but the struggle of syntax and the difficulty of words:

Tikhon, I can't speak, you kept saying
I cannot speak (p.80)

This contains one of the few purely Russian references in the text which westerners will be unlikely to know: Tikhon was the last patriarch of the Orthodox church who tried unsuccessfully to mediate between the church and the new communist regime; the reference to the hundred-headed city in another poem (p.24) is to the church council or synod which reduced the power of the patriarch in the 18th century. There are perhaps some other allusions to her native country, such as the 'white nights' in one poem, but in general Glazova's work does not depend on understanding location or geographical or cultural setting in the way that some other poets' does.

The compression of the writing, however, borders on the unsayable. Sometimes, for me, a line or phrase simply does not come across: for example 'a ringing stream in the knee jar' (p.25) or 'how we mixed' (p.29). This may be just me, or the inescapable import tariff one pays on translation, though I suspect it is actually a function of the compression of the original, the pushing up to a certain limit. But at other times that compression works superbly, as in one of her finest short poems:

will come and raise up
the broken in stone
the greek to me
and hang it on the wind
what: the unfurlgrass

*

will not. come or raise. (p.31)

It is not just the density of the imagery that is striking here, but the abrupt halts: (what; will not) and a reflexivity so entwined with the objects of reflection as to be almost inseparable.

It is difficult to place Glazova's work, but one striking feature is its imagery. To understand the nature of images, we have to go back to Aristotle's distinction between essential and accidental attributes. Essential attributes are those which are necessary to the definition or identity of something; accidental ones are non-essential or additional. Few philosophers now espouse this kind of essentialism, but we can substitute the idea of habitual use or meaning found in the later Wittgenstein of the *Investigations*: 'what we call descriptions are instruments for particular purposes'.

Images involve accidental attributes; they highlight aspects of and links between things that we do not usually notice or consider. In this way they enrich our world, and give it a much more associative, complex texture than that of everyday functionality. They create a kind of delicate, often elusive filigree of meaning, providing a suprising and even reassuring sense of the connectedness of things. Some of Glazova's images are of this kind

the white cloth of a wave at rest (p.46)

and the shadow stretches from the staff (p.19)

coiled on the moist
inside or to be precise with the precision
of a coincidence you look in that direction (p.20)

However, such images typically leave in place the essences or identities of things, the world we recognise, and in that sense are ultimately representational. Glazova's work goes beyond this, creating a world of pure attributes and qualities: in a word, abstraction.

a ringing stream in the knee jar
a ringing
not heard by a silver hammer
on a gold anvil,

the ringing,
the knee,
not heard

from the golden apple of real summer (p.25)

we have so bent the clear sea
that only night is inside, so we can,
in the dark, in the neon light,
see air and light (p.37)

 And it is this which perhaps shows most clearly her deep immersion in phenomenology, because for phenomenologists, the very idea of essence is also to be subjected to its unsparing analysis, and our construction of meaning is just one more feature of the world which has to be de-constructed; after all, how could something so basic be exempt? Glazova does not just enrich the textures of our world; the very urge to relate, construct or associate is caught, held, turned back on itself; the poetic equivalent of Husserl's 'presuppositionless philosophy'. And it is this which ultimately places her in a poetics of consciousness rather than a poetics of experience, reflexive rather than reflective, because the very notion of experience contains assumptions which in her writing are themselves exposed and laid bare. There are affinities with abstract painting.

 Without knowing Russian, it is difficult to locate her work in terms of what is going on there currently. Glazova's second language is German, and there are possible connections there too. Certainly, her poetry brings something quite different and even alien into the anglophone bloodstream, and Shearsman is to be congratulated for this opening onto another poetic culture, manifest in some of its other published translations also.

However, it is the individuality of this work that strikes me most; I can think of little other contemporary poetry that is so objective in its concern with things, yet somehow personal, as this.

Geoffrey Squires

TWICE UNDER THE SUN

* * *

in the sunflower—
that is: in the sun and in flower—
so are we alive

then only do seeds ripen
when the sun burns their skins,
shields them from the sun with hard night
and no longer milk—
dark-pale oil
fills them.

then only lift my head toward the light
and shield it
with your face
as shade.

* * *

not lighter not farther north
but finer and sharper
flaking away from pain
a little lens, trembling
when held to the light, like a drop
in water.

terrible to hold to the light
in the index and thumb
of a skinned grape
a small heart.

when suspended from every finger
swings a world.

* * *

shelled from the pod
in the earth
from rocky pores
and the roe of moles in red shafts

splitting into
rungs a two-tailed
bean whip
climbs the staff of Tiresias
and the face reaches to

stop the sun?

or not separate
the two shoots, but weave
a basket from the stunned snakes.
gather the golden grains
from the dark pods which fall
with a soft thud
to the earth.

and the shadow stretches from the staff.

* * *

no lighter than shade
set like a fig
with its ovary
wingless and dry
inside,
coiled on the moist
inside or to be precise: with the precision
of a coincidence you look in that direction,
palms above your head,
and behind the green ribbed wall of your roof
you know one thing.

how he'd set himself free,
if at midnight
the black well of his mind bloomed a hand from his hoof
setting like a fig
or a sky: with the shade inside.

* * *

into what one can stay—
it will flow and spill out
and freeze and shiver now steam—
if you stand up and lean stubborn and dip your hot hand
only your tracks will stretch
till there's no trace.

to stay the hands. to breathe from your palm the print.
to erase yourself after yourself.

ITHACA

turtledoves hide in trees,
hard to breathe without stutter,
like a harpy in a tree sitting
in a shaggy fleece
I have spun and spun
and drawn out what I'd like to forget.

you can't tell who is brooding
who.

much is born in nests
which none will see in a dream,
and you'll miss
how winged things turn into ghosts when re-told
like they had never been.

who will teach me to breathe if taken,
not at his word, but at breath;
read this tale of nests in which no one is sailing
and the big eyes of horror
or maybe a child
keep a kernel from being born,
no matter if it's a nut, a bird or a planet?

and your fear sails inside a whole sphere to Ithaca,
and you sit in it, dimly hoping
that Icarus, wind or a swan
will escape from the knot in your throat.

* * *

go down
careful and light
through the bladder air
through the throat
into the deep breach, the sharp air

a blaze and dust and in the smoke

dig a hole.
keep silent the weight of the worn lung away.
I.
bury it.

in the holehole
horsewhip the smoky wail
of the septagod, pour the ink
and smile with all seven lips—

      sight or unseen

      long story or short

      when is all said or done

—no
the sharp-shooting air
earth.

* * *

to be no angel
honey and tar
close
your eyes, wings, pores

where an open book reads
unmoved from the ending
about hard feathers.

a cloud sat down
hundred-headed like a city,
you want to set foot
and it's wet, and you torture
the implacable checkers, a handkerchief.

tie it all up in a bundle
and carry away
the uncovered night and one core
which you will sow and reap, sow and reap.

* * *

for Trevor Joyce

a ringing stream in the knee jar
a ringing
not heard by a silver hammer
on a gold anvil,

the ringing,
the knee,
not heard

from the golden apple of real summer.

the prints over streams are so tangled
the joints are swollen
from which

the legs of tributary willows grow
to bear. while the crown wants to lean
into the cold mouth's knee.
(you have wandered the streams for so long
it's been apples hammering their ringing.)

wants to lean where it's ringing glass.

* * *

as palm to palm
not to be brought beyond
the border
of the three axes of light
two halves not to be made one.

as in the middle
exactly not in half
a twice-wound heart lies inside itself, a chamber, cased quartet.

I don't see the murky crystal lens
beyond the pupil—only the blue sky, the dark well, level days.
if there's a middle, it's not through the mouth or the sacrum her
    cord grows.
an opaque shadow between apple halves
under a lowered eyelid, under a lowered branch.

* * *

close your eyes and watch
small blue veins
cover an orange leaf: an unmixing of fire.

not before a shop window but in front of bars
we'll feed
a hungry liver
of the firing dark: not with wine or with blood
not a beak
but white paper like breathing out.

and be warm
hiding hands in the glove of each other.

* * *

for Svetlana K.

in a small foreign nut
cave, wearing
Empedocles' slippers, without a mirror, with one, but in the dark.

hornless he descends
and cannot descend,
the avalanche speeds things up before Sisyphus,
a bunch of grape snails lives in Tantalus' teeth.

the way the black the blue sea has retreated
and the desert sifted into a salt-shaker's little body.
sleep around me, silk hill, forest growing pink,
sleep, and like her who lays silkworm with the sheep,
I shall make notches about a pale blush.

* * *

how we mixed.
dividing: honey, milk, a kid, his mother's.
how we mixed, knowing the taste and the limit
how we mixed is poison to him who does not
know where the taste and the limit are,
and the limit.

how we mix.
dividing: honey, a kid, a cup, our measure.
how we mix is poison to him who does not
know the limit
and the measurelessness of measure.

teach me to know. teach our measure to us.

* * *

heavy oil unglowing honey
you tell me in my skin and mouth: "the nape" and the fingers
      are in the hair

I hold the shy bunch
berries maybe or silent beasts

if they fall, will they break?—silence

"shoulder" is close "back" is closer
matting together and rolling
now say "you're a hand to me"
I will knead the wax and not crush the stirring
beads I am holding and olive honey
will lick their lips

* * *

will come and raise up
the broken in stone
the greek to me
and hang it on the wind
what: the unfurlgrass

*

will not. come or raise.

* * *

birch and pine grow
from the same root.
bark wraps a pitch lump
of thick buried summer
hand seals as from eye.

this resin, quiet, slowly fluid in itself.

★ ★ ★

a girl in gloves
is flying a falcon
in a kitchen garden.
the falcon flies high,
sees far,
comes back quick,
and she looks at the wings
wider than two rhubarb leaves
and the figures they make.
this is her lesson.

***

in a clear wood
by a lopsided stump
a shudder
crawls through the moss—
inopportune feet,
inconspicuous face,
looking for a root
from which a rainbow
will grow, the other
end into golden
water, and her wood is
of lace.

* * *

black she eats
pearls my pearl
on your breast
my pearl on your wrist.
eat on.
when the light
from the end
comes to the beginning
all the druses are open to us.

* * *

nine months later
the mouse is in labor
a mountain range
crawls toward the horizon
crowds on the shore.

let's breathe
be
not a mountain or mouse
clouds crawl in the sky
and worms in the earth
so leave the sky to them
who are of the sky

* * *

we have bent the wall so
that all doors are outside
and inside is the sea
and all rivers flow down
red carpets, down which you'd sail
fleet-footed like the truth.

every design is a flower
if you see through the stem.
we have so bent the clear sea
that only night is inside, so we can,
in the dark, in the neon light,
see air and light.

***

twist a rope into kinks
lie down in a dark place and wait
till a noose traps
sip air from it
through a straw
a ray between boards
decoy it with folds in a cloth
and a broken mirror
this is a room hunt
for wild light

* * *

blue.
like the sky like the sea like the sound wave
I am silent with, I have agreed not to sing
as we talk.

blue like lightning, the smell
like ozone. electricity like a crackling letter
you read in low light at midnight.

blue, hidden under the tongue, in the well of a pupil,
sweeping like a bird

I'm not after. no birdcatcher nor an augur.
let the birds listen for fish, fish for birds.
as you are sound, so is my rest.

* * *

the way I hear you, you hear.
lay fingers on my mouth
I will
lay fingers on your fingers
and so
now speak,
word for word and not give and take.
I stand because now is the time
you are teaching yourself
not to stand
not to wait.

* * *

as retina into retina
not to throw net into water
but to throw net into net
net into net
and water
aerial water
over the stream over paper
not mist not bog
aster of two not entwined
but transparent
to each other
twang solar tangles

* * *

like that time when not I to me, not you-you,
not not-you, not not-not-you,
when you,
when on the third, on the fourth attempt
you said 'you,'
so we've just locked
my not mute not not mute,
me and you,
we've locked lips.

how—so,
so I know
not what I do
or do not know
that I will know,
that I will forever know,
that I will forever know.

* * *

you know what color
the sail must be
not to burst in the solar wind?
from what quiet I pull this silk,
from what spiders I take it.
how many holes I leave for the extra sunbeams.

a black sail brings profit,
a red one offspring.
faces tucked into white winding-sheets come the enemy the
        brief guest.
yellow velvet is stretched on the vessel of the sick rich.

rushed like the seconds of eyelashes
colorless like the bare body
nobody's like our sailboat the sail I weave you.

* * *

"getting harder to go through doors into doors"—
you forget which.
take the steps then turn, make a turn, don't
miss a turn or skip a beat like a watch:
in the direction.

you can't say left with your right hand,
you can't but right.
air is lined with the right rectitude but
when you breathe in it tends left
and when out, is through.

* * *

through the sand through the ligneous
crossing sinews
somewhere of stone somewhere at dusk and through
the murmur from
from the thrown open like windows transpiring
almost aloud from the
keys
under the word
"turn"

stirs the green thick

and don't bother to ask the big straw
where they buried the truck.
turn this to the left and it will foam,
right, flow. another man's hard hat hangs from the aspen.

here's a bucket of sweat from your feet,
let go of the amulet and the case.
roots and stones aren't a break
or fire, and will not heal.

* * *

nearer than seam or skin
deeper than air
a reverse tree
plays beast
the white cloth of a wave at rest

slowly you drop, a proud was-become,
to your knees
there grows your sandal-bush
through the sky, soil-up on bare roots.
there marches your very slow bush.
there I eat with my lips from the saucer: breath, clearing,
lemon.

there I will lie.
let my blanket be
crooked earth, sticky time.
let the unemployed creature
grow into me through the seam and skin through the air,
I will muzzle it, make it graze.

* * *

the sun cracked on your lips
and cracked open the eyes of your nipples
unblinking
spin sun thread from them
threshold to threshold
through the hard labor of light
the fraction of ice in your hair
I am tired in your belly
in the sun in the burned-out burn
of thawed ash

* * *

is it time to get out
if you're going to drop it anyway,
unawares, if you're going to break a blue column of water.
there, they strike the pavement.

you nod your meaningless head, are a horse,
an ass, not living but drawn,
you measure air with your back.

mixed with black, water gives—
when you drink or when air—a picture.
no, not you: this is I, but two,
and one day I'll get fire and water mixed up.
how many times can a town square tear.
your head flows under the stones.

★ ★ ★

I have no fear of fighting,
of the word,
give over your bubble.

so we don't let it slip and get lost,
but how much does one need,
he walks, trips, falls.
or is full of sun from the puddle
or—you can't distinguish what's reflected—
smear the rainbow
'round his eyes, they never wanted for brains.
sharp turns,
spheres in the eyes,

head spinning
in squares,
right, let's go.

* * *

something like that
lying someplace
so you can't tell
seems to glow

begin to speak and you freeze;
go on and you have no blanket;
incensed, you finish off,
spit at the tinder

* * *

the candle's met his match
the butter his scabbard
air fell through a pit
and she's eating him

the local of all places
is waltzing around his place
the wind whets a blade
on own skin

you rake light like chestnuts on an open flame
shadow becomes glass in a shaky windowpane

* * *

you will never come home
wherever you go,
all open doors,
all closed doors,
all are yours—and a law in each
that a key opens
and locks,
and behind each a glowing garden
or the dark or a stuffy cupboard,
and you pull a thread from your soul
through your mouth and mark the road,
how could you believe,
many-eyed, bald, that you'd ever arrive.

* * *

dust of ashes
do ashes have dust?
white-hot motes
to burn hands
(as to kiss
an iron trunk in the cold)

in an urn
an icicle flame
ice eats at the leaves
edges run
the letters are wax

under your lights
not a plain but a hole
in the hole a casket
in the casket a hole
in the hole a slit
poked-out air (eye)

look
look at us
look you won't see the glass
body (no corpse) through

* * *

on the threshold.
twist my foot and fall to the feet?
little by little, or so it seems,
payback time gives high
way (instead of feet)
to the pentacorn hands.

boy, do you stretch.
like the road is your best sheet.
like the road you run to a thick picket fence
and sit.
pricking in your stumble.

* * *

what shall we pelt water with?
stones (that's stupid), hands (hard)
maybe force but it pulls the palms,
in a boat, with an oar, we'll row, for the tracks on the water, a
    wedge,
of cranes,
like docks beaten into the heart.

and it shivers.
like a thing of glass in a clock shop
it goes, it stands
in the window,
not before it,
water showing through stone.

pelt water with that.
stone. let it shiver, stones, water,
you'll know how it won't be:
an oar with only one foot;
circles across the surface.

* * *

one cut the pages, glued them back together
never disturbing a line,
ate a cigarette butt not his own,
spit three times into open doors.
took leave.
said so but turned back,
never said it but asked us to pass it on: it's all right,
I thought it would be like new.

* * *

is standing at the crossroads
and won't move
wink as you might.

the air tosses
a red wrapper
and the gate is red.

no turning, no saying: let's,
there is no stop here.
a tram passes.
won't budge.

* * *

wait, not like this.
what are you waiting for, beached,
why do you think I can't see?

don't look, walk away.
think of something simpler for yourself.
you know—ripe field, plowed field, sugar loaf,
or stuck in the throat?

you take your hands off your belly, reach for your mouth.
now, there you have it, blue water,
blue water,
black sail, red mark

* * *

a gull's getting old
is already begging
a broken tree
begging fire

a starving what
by the water's edge
slippery head
spinning

look
a rag on a treadmill,
a worm squirrel;
he knew and was fallen asleep

* * *

the books have bedsores
shelves on the floor
chair unsteady
lay it down or off with the back

every cloud
comes to him who waits
do not beat clock hands
my stainless coat

what, what time is it, now?
the table flinched through its face
somehow unbearable, brothers
erode the bottom with lime

* * *

I get a letter and it spills threads.
a bundle of clothes falls out,
vile, worn, with fuzz balls,
I don't like these burrows, fur bellows,
why dump all this on me?
you rub your pencil
against wool,
stealthily—a bad habit—
the worse, the better I know
how you write this,
and I chew this wool from your own sheep head with a human sigh.

* * *

lamplight falls into no hand.
in the book a face cools
shaved off by a hair
as a second
shaves a zero off the time.

in this book one cannot but read
not of someone's path around the lamp.
no lamp nor the sun but an eye
revolves there.
it reads with its hands
the tracks which the light leaves behind.

* * *

apples, a couple, are hanging
among a split wall.
nowhere to fall: the weight is gone
into the heart of the cliff.
the wilding is tearing
away at the rot in the crack,
both branches bent with the sound.

if the inside of the fog is soft,
let's fall there.

* * *

sailor halt. rider where do you ride?
eastward. westward. southward. north.
four ways forks the road.
in the compass, mercury's curdled.
poles.
belts.
axes.
clearings.
circles.

* * *

a fish standing in a flood changes,
grows hooves in the fins maybe
or maybe its body abates.
the sky looks inside it
and the water grows thin.
more mouth, only
swept away is
the teething.
the shoalfish.

a steed not bearable
of which all depth
grows no shallower
hones the bottom
of water unmade
and unsaddled is he

—I will go now and ride o! a tandem of fishes

* * *

various thoughts
leave the head
and do a headstand together, span to span.

where the sky is ajar
an even cloud glows.

from it fall
wool, feather, salt,
ash, nitre.

* * *

accidental ascent belighted,
a black lump detaches, rolls down the slope,
shadow teased into grass.

the wall-eyed bottom comes crawling from under my feet,
I can recall how a branch
with a cottonwood mouse breaks off.

no, this is only the eye of my son,
insomniac in the hall and the night.
the eye which I remember by ear.

* * *

through a steamship
through the house
up the steps
an easy death? a she-I
never looked for such profits.
took I-her arm in her arms, drank her fill
from her palm. didn't touch the snow
though hands grew black in the smoke.

she-I watched the near moon on the window,
a weary cloud lay in it-her, who'd notice the wrong space.
nottheplace where the grass wouldn't grow
felt like howling but only grew over with arms.
to have no time to die to
grate yourself a crater below the desert and never explode.

the sea boiling in it-her sank to the bottom
a face barely made it, was born, opened its eyes in the sun that
    remained,
closed them,
counted the coins with her hands, not you, that she-other. what
    did you see?

what did I see? thick, indigo-blue green grapes.
sudden moonlight on steps and stones.
a raw wet as it crept from barrels and days.
she-I got poisoning from the drinking water
as they were pouring my glass.
who can tell, in a day or two or stone and night
I may not want it,
a mooncrawler finally looming at me through the vapor.

* * *

in the dark you're the same.
remember the gray sky, extinguished thread, and
I shivered as I waited.
forgot, drank water, table stained: somebody been smoking.
wrought hair from the bulb with no light,
on the pillow, to scrape the cheek with.

dim; were sitting. I think so, yes.
caught another's leg on the edge,
are you joking? "for the night is thick."
listen, all right, lie, lie, but at least with feeling:
words got soaked, couldn't speak.
covered a dried-up drop of wine with a handkerchief—
ashamed, that's what you are, or maybe afraid.

I still have batwing shadows about my head,
that's after that flight, been spinning, head swimming.
let's take the fire exit? no, you say
no, no, no, I can't. you be the one to live.
me, I'm kind of not here. dust.

go shake it out, though not into a bag,
I'll sit here for a while. anyway you can't see in this dark
how last night they burnt stumps.
cream at the cut, cremation,
as they sipped, no, snipped the dairy plums.

FIRST DAY

sleeprunning deer
a slant careering
of a slowest flood
and a forest fire
all fled
a halt
high time to start a chronicle
first entry: ate offal fur cones
(cedars fell
scanning rain
and a kite askance)

MANUSCRIPT IN A BOTTLE

death is sealed in a capsule
it's tail-spun into flesh with a corkscrew
as an ovary into a bud
drawn tight with a belly-button
I blossom and
a slow nenuphar
I blossom
I am lost on a bottom
of bottle green
welded with wax

HE-HORSE

a seahorse
tearing with pain
gives birth through his belly button
to semi-transparent spawn in the coral
where nereids shelter their estrus at easter
they of sexless wombs and mocking:
art thou a steed or no steed?
steed thou, no steed?
sobbing, the seahorse
stains baby hobbies with seed

* * *

here
flow the fractions: wood, foam, rusty, shag, city, square, screen:
see, without paper they live like they aren't things:
filling the face, palm to palm, a self-
fluttering eye
on a close
line.

you fell with your face to the glass but you see
it
differently now.
like those waves were breaking in you not in the sea you swam,
even black pain broken off
with a line of
light?

a sepulchre by the sea a glass tub out of which
someone poured the baby with the water
you sit
wrapped up
and afraid of the water like lime.

no
lime, no.
of mountain silk, asbestos,
I wove
the cloth
for you,
no hair
shirt. I am no Delilah.

* * *

the wind, the wind!
from the centuries
from the deep of the mute
from the hidden from sight—no: just across-the-across

on the stalk
do not quite break off
do not break the stare
do not let and do not not let go

across cherries
black earth tillage
till it is so late
later than the white nights or black days

is where we shall meet.
in the rush of wind we shall listen
to the skin-to-skin speech
of air stones.

* * *

a woman in heels walks by.
somewhere, a window slams shut.
we have started the car
and now wait while they wash the balcony.
hi how are you, I say, o head o knee!
a mahogany log is what you'll get, not a table.
black furniture, white walls, woman.
a woman in flowers.

we bend our head because we're long acquainted.
the third bottle has started.
she says: well, hello then.
no, not the one in heels and in flowers
but the one leaning on the log.
and checking her elbow like her watch.

I'm leafing through, weakly, feigning indifference.
if anything happens, run, run.
I'm thinking: should I call, should I ask,
say, well what's up with you? slept yourself out yet?
what do you mean never went to bed? but no: too strange.
you think: by tonight they'll be done with the threshing
without me,
leave no bones to pick. slips of empty paper, film.

right.
all of time till tomorrow.
midnight still to come.
you'd put a chair on your head,
rearrange the jar with the flowers, after all we're related.
they'll get the joke.
they crochet, embroider, set out plants,
and, with a knife, knock the top off an egg in the morning.

wiped her face with a towel. she's almost in tears.
and what was this for? well, I ask her, let's play?
but she's at it again.

black walls, the woman is white, wrapped up in bedclothes, asleep.
shoes in the corner, punished.
watching a dream about how they are broken.
well and you? well nothing: sitting, waiting. mending.
both woke up in the morning as though there'd been nothing.
dust turning under the bed, fair weather.
says, to kill you would not be enough. and what do I care—
as long as there's black, white, red, even odd.

* * *

you are flying apart:
shiny winds hibernate
in the once-warm sty.
nightingale swine tell you get lost, blight!
we'd rather starve than eat human.

the winds will blow down the sky. it's the swine, gorged on peas.
you know I know. the blue sky lay there on the bottom.
we kept kissing the sky and we waited
in the ditch and we rolled like the swine in the cold
grass. their bellies grew heavy and grass lay below us.

that's what the green-bottle in me buzzed in my head once.
she-I was reading a book that said nothing of this.
he-I didn't read, it-I never droned, but a balcony cornice snaps
into the white echo here,
and a rootless hair, a white hair, never sheared my
ear, the cronk of answerless hooves.

gray matter engorges a blue gleaming beak.
let's have no blood, though! I'm begging you, let's be water
        and water.
having divided in two. divided the empty along the
two. we'll drink as if knifing as they are knifing me.

horses whine. that was mice. never fear, she-dear,
that's, he-my sweet, the wind that sobs in my dark.
we'll sing, howling, and cry, child, in the night after drowning,
we'll be a virgin and set
off for the hungry den.

hogs on the head.
kindly, taciturn hands. that's how you'd knife my backbone,

seek your backbone, you slept a long time, fallen into the heart
 as ruins
will fall into crispy sound
the day of the mangy hog's last neigh.

he-I have said this loud word forevermore.
forevermore, she-I said: and one must believe the word.
we knifed open the lids of the bleak finnish sphinx,
and in the bay stood—full of a spanish red—mange.

let us shut! tell me nothing of sound! I cannot
hear! o thick bile of gold,
he-I am tired.
he-I have waited for you. by the wall, propped up,
she-I have slept.
he-I am tired to death, defecating upon the bare backs of the rocks—
and on that.

* * *

>   *for Anna Khasin*

tower or fort?
a question familiar to any anne
the fort the higher the lung ascends
the tower the tighter the bone's forced apart

tower and fort. any
lightweight news will find weight.
head spins ascent
of the tower though of stone feels like jelly.

you know, maybe we've got the average
as with a sheer stone as with the head
to measure the angles and fly the distance
run fort and tower down to the base
and run off in peace down the rope

* * *

and in this spectacle of doves
too there's a place for us, do you think?
who will give it up? who in time
have become a sign of the commonplace.
they whose ghost divided among the one
comes no more, has become a ghost.

oh, the things one dreams under
this orphanage sky!
in passing from this and that: I'm listening, yes.
you pacific dregs in a plastic shell
speak for me. whispers of foam on beer.

shall not be banished, even to the sea:
you can ring a man at the seaside these days.
to drink o to drink tap brine
like a poppy or memory, shut me up
Tikhon, I can't speak, you kept saying
I cannot speak.

* * *

can't put two words together—
think twice,

invent how a woman
lifts her skirt,
how strips of cloud
are seen from the shade, and in the threads
of a cloth of looks
stands silence,

and light and the sea
part if told to part,
open like wet lips,
not a word, not a sound.

think of wanting to throw
a stone into the water for a splash.
birds think less.

* * *

pouring wine on the scale
from tilted glasses
water from an underground spring
—as the wind blew the snow from the tops—
never letting a crystal touch their water
never lighting a fire
who drank from the scale? a pair, dead or none?
quietly the pans sway
pouring liquid light into one another.

* * *

it flows and smashes. you don't budge:
not because you're held down by the sheet of glass
or by dragging or by way of staying.

flows and smashes against the glass, this means
don't stand, you will become plum.
you're paying well for your sleep, dream.

three strokes from the edge
through many people,
an orange sail. never seen one like that?

and the shred plunged: I would look, hand raised from the sun,
but a swum-by body has choked you,
that's the anchor dropped.

COMPASS

from the bluff to the northern fur coat,
between the goat and Tauris
in the tongue of belladonna,
when three times, wolf-like,
nipples glimmered,
chew your lyre up, you,
and digest it
into a single-sex magnet—
may you be writing
as in a dream, this side and that
and dreaming and not.

on what ship and how
will she fall asleep,
Iphigenia
in Hyperborea, to wake
in a ditch and read
passers-by's north
in their palms?

* * *

take a template and cover
the boggy pigeonhouse, the wolfpen,
with prints of pigeons,
where beasts
take solid food, don't break blue teeth
on the thicket of shingles,
on speldings or on a trunk.

and gather, gather the cuttings
into bald pelts,
and shingle,
shingle and
cuttings of the ground
of the heavens and their loose clashing windows.

take a template and cover.

* * *

light fell
hit the ground, became light.

from it jumped
one as though from fear
with a big foot but little air
step by step along the field edge by stops and starts
past the hill of turtles
crushing their shells for Achilles' wrath—

and there she
hit light.

her heart leapt out, along the path, beyond the switch
pointing:
"look, light, what I've got on and in is in tatters."
and the runner with her poised neck
from which the tattered ball escaped—eyes empty,
she's arrived—

stop, tombstone,
I'll roll free of you
to measure pits and heights.

* * *

unrest;
the lunatic
hides his ears;
the word crowns and strikes;

and strikes
open water from the crown of his head;
from the bitter lips
runs
rich soap.

* * *

an egyptian octopus god
holding shadows of corals;
a blue glow around his grey head
misty in dull water;
a skate sheltering
claret streams from the sun:
so memory
older than reefs
streams from under a sonorous heart,
whose pulse is an eon
and silence an earthquake.

* * *

snakes swim
into streams
under a berm,
news on each tail;
eternal dust on each eye;

and the currents are covered with branches of slender trees,
where a dromedary walks,
rocking like a street: left and right,
and a bike wheel
spins, sand snakes
under the thick tire, the burden sags,
a dull day over subterranean currents
is bound with the saliva of snakes.

* * *

a traveller with a dog
took my hand
and across a footbridge
over a gully
full of flowers,
and through a thicket,
tangled wind in the treetops,
soft leaves under the trees

and the dew on the brush,
and the traveller with the dog,
his face hidden,
by the footbridge and here a path, there dirt,
has led me to people,
and I speak to them, and they hear,
their air my air.

* * *

a fisherman pulls
a lame old boat
to the shore
with a hook on a pole.
inside it is
a drawing
sealed in oiled canvas.
he could not yet make a flint tinderbox,
basalt spatulae,
but he knew how to saw limestone
and make paper prints of plant reflections.

* * *

sent—

first
shoots from a bow
then an arch and an arch
from dark water
along a hard palm stalk
as ivy
leaved in winter.
along the stalk of a golden,
along the stalk, along
the coconut palm, shedding
tears because he cannot fall asleep
and shed a hundred o
hundred of
nuts.

sent

instead of the green-black ink not a leaf
not a leaf
from the coconut palm,
first a nut's ghost,
in the end
a lone leaf with a print of a stone
or hard knuckles
and of a sign
no sign.

* * *

from slant lashes—
shadows of voice, fires of the dark,
blind from fatigue—
speechlessness sat braiding
hair, a tangled
long-wearing crown
not of her own but of so much hair
for the long ploughing
of the shrill bearded full seabed.

between day, between crowns and the end of the world
the furrow is crooked.
the furrow is straight.
owls of tails between guard towers of grey boughs,
speechlessness into burrows. between them
and the hollows of the earth
where the root sings,

with your flint-worn dusty hands extend
the red print of fire:
I'll keep it longer than I will my word.

* * *

my faith sleeps
under cottonwood,
don't wake it god
don't wake it white
don't spin the wool.

but the strings
reach
through tomorrow, today,
—to spin silver felt.

to spin from white light
an elaborate coverlet
in which you can't see a face,
in which a face, faith is.

Troy

hands erect the ruins on their own.
from paper, homes, from books, hills, and
I'll break mines of plates,
lay rivers of scarves.
off the street, dirty,
one I'll wash in foaming waters,
pour wine over, encircle with honey, lay a stone:
here will be a city.

Troy, untouched.
your stone has been washed from the fire
into my home.

Poppy and Somn

i. a mechanical brain

a multilayer residue softly formed on the blue seafloor: a reptile's third eyelid, slowly peeling until a complete mutation of the eye occurred, and a bent floater of an amphibian; discarded segments of a snake's imperfect nervous and digestive systems; vegetable soil and animal humus; solar plexus of human cerebral palsy and distended hydrocephalic sexual organs of lower primates: protein shells and chains slipped (sloughing, chipping, relin-quishing, shirking, estranging the maternal object) through the soft and dense plasma of translucid brine to the very blue bottom. there they folded themselves in thin sheets, smelting, mixing and coupling with each other, losing characteristics, changing in composition, trading shreds of amino acids, until they turned into a uniform, agile biomass which began to breathe sour liquefied subaquatic air, release lisping and rustling bubbles of waste products, lift and lower its broad cool chest, feed and swallow the deep fish. dark, upward-brightening water continued to sway above this heaving mass, squeezing the blue and yellow bottom with the pressure of several atmospheres. buckling and pressing its loose pulsating flesh into the sand, the broody lap of the ocean slowly throbbed, contracted, expanded, scooped in red ocean sand with its giant snail foot, weakly phosphorescing with a gaseous blue of subaqueous luminescence. gilded inside with shell crumb and starfish sheath, the slow sub-ocean womb's fallopian tubes stirred and flared in the cool fluid, swaying like enormous sea anemones in the tide; the water that swirled at their openings was saturated with salt, seaweed fragments, powdered lobster shells, seed of monoecious fish, seahorse roe and filaments of tangle. a funnel gradually formed at the opening of each tube; one spun clockwise, the other counterclockwise. embroiled objects remained in the eddies; new fragments of flesh were pulled, packed, squeezed in, ingrown and stuck together into flabby pale-motley spherical lumps. guided by the swaying, wide-open sleeves of the tubes, the lumps, which had become heavy, dense, overgrown with matter, slowed their spinning inside the giant cuffs to smooth measured cycles. tides swung the resilient muscular photosynthetic tissue, and it vibrated in response, itself causing waves, tsunamis, typhoons, broad high and sucking low tides. the moon sent a livid glint through the water column, wild meat-red shadows lying deep in her craters. under the influence of sunlight the lumps began to form nuclei. they stored heat, giving rise to a hot epithelium and compressing the matter in their centers, so that its finest particles fractured and caused a chain reaction in each other, swarming and radiating and re-absorbing their own heat, born of dry sunlight and wet glimpse of the moon. the nuclei became red-hot. their dark glow broke through the translucent matter of the ovarian lumps. the inner spheres caused their outer case to vitrify, harden and crack. the rotation came nearly to rest; undercurrents husked the burnt fringe off the ovaries and carried it, dissolved, into the upper layers of the hydrosphere. the completed red egg cells hatched from their dark shells. the soft abyssal womb shuddered pinkly and began to pull them into its bulging gaping center. both egg cells stretched into ovals and stuck to the sleeves; near the very entrance to the porous, pale palpus- and cilia-covered sea womb, the cells collided, causing an underwater explosion which sent a wave rolling along the seafloor. radiating in the blue and yellow regions of the spectrum, the cells merged into a single small solid red pore shaped like a six-bowed sun. the womb sucked this seed in; the sleeves fell limply down on her papillate, ciliate breast. their throes soon ceased; the sleeves rotted off and turned into plankton; the womb slowly swallowed and digested it. wisps of moonlight and the heavy foliage of sunlight were still being absorbed by the bulging womb. when it had swelled to an ample reef (significantly raising the sea-level), the moon, fixed in its full phase, grew threefold over the course of several lunar months. the red shadows in its craters' cavernous structures now lay deeper and sharper, resembling venous-dark clots. the center of the lunar face showed a deep crack with a noticeable rhomboid orifice in the middle. the black crown which had formed around the moon now and then ejected snaking protuberances which rushed about the sky like rabid eels. during the eclipse, when the solar disk was fully overcast by the lunar shadow, a flow of burning lava shot through the rhomboid crater from the tumultuous nucleus of the moon and, thickening in space into an oblong metallic drop that tapered toward its tail, careered toward the earth. once in the ocean waters, the hot cosmic sperm cell slowed its motion, cooling, hissing and piercing the water column. passing through marine animals' bodies and blundering into cliffs, the sperm cell kept changing its newly pliable form, and by the time it was drawn into the orifice of the panting sea womb, it resembled a double serrated sprocket, held together by a girdle of ball bearings. the womb swallowed the sprocket convulsively and began to slowly contract and descend toward the bottom. there, in the sepulchral underwater dusk, the sprocket merged with the six-pointed pore. from time to time electric skates occluded the womb and shot with blue arches of weak current through it. deep-water mollusks encrusted the entrance; later it became overgrown with yellow coral, so as not to open before its time. falling onto the arch and rays of the soft and yielding pore, the sprocket immediately got rid of the first layer (which dissolved in the sour white blood secreted by the hexacron), then of the ball-bearings (one by one they disappeared with a mute splash inside the circle, aiming for the very center), and finally the remaining upper layer together with drops of lubricant and engine grease ran all over the surface of the swollen cell, forming a protective layer, a placenta for the future embryo. when the cell had completely filmed over, the violent process of division and growth began. small shuttles darted back and forth, a double spiral thread vibrated, the tissue darned itself and grew, needles jumped about, sewing together corners, cranks chattered and froze on the up-beat, the spindle spun, gathering the thread, the clamps on the spinning loom banged, the blades of scissors sped by, cutting, re-shaping, turning out flesh, scraps of which dissolved into threads again and were re-used. soon the frontal lobes were ready, but the cerebellum remained barely marked out in red basting-thread. unstitching the blood in the innermost womb and discharging a puddle onto the loose uterine floor, the needles were replaced by pegs pulling a long burgundy thread from the pool to the embryo and winding translucent red convolutions around the iron structures, the brain's skeleton. the rear sections of the brain were already phosphorescing with yellowish consciousness; raw electricity was running along the annulated motley wires of the nerves; here and there a short circuit shot through the water with a small hiss. a wide board, spangled like a miniaturist's palette with multi-colored nodules on both sides, grew into the space between the frontal lobes. shuttles with low-buzzing spools leapt up to it cautiously to deliver a violet, orange, or blue drop; sometimes a shuttle became entangled in the bare live wires—then an electric discharge occurred amid dry crackling noise, and the charred shuttle leapt off to the bottom, where it would melt in the thickening puddle. products of hydrolysis swirled about in the dark green water. stretched on thick cables made of securely braided eye nerves and optical fibers in durable cases, the mechanical brain was swaying with the benthal waves. translucent platinum reinforced with ganglia formed the glimmering cortex and subcortex. the uterine opening, overgrown with rose-yellow coral, began to distend; the corals crumbled off and were separated from the womb by eddies, which the uterus began to suck in with a loud noise. the brain received a centripetal impulse from their strong and pliant currents and slowly began to rotate around an imaginary axis which pierced the opening of the uterus. during the rotation, the cables gently loosened the clamps by which the brain was attached, and the warty organic suckers released the brain. a forceful whirlpool formed, the brain spinning ever faster in it; the uterine opening dilated, the brain shot through it, ripping out a powerful tail of water, sand, organic and mechanical surplus; the sea lap collapsed into a pile of scrap metal behind him, burying the parasites of the meaty placenta under a pile of worn rusty lumps of flesh. drilling through the ocean surface and causing turbulence and storms, the brain hurtled toward the proto-shore. a huge wave threw him onto dry land; his wet surface blazing in the sun, seaweed that clung to him stretching back into the water. having landed, the brain began to snake with shoots and to send them into the soil and water. photosynthetic activity throbbed underneath the membrane; the translucent lining of the subcortex reflected blue images. two mechanical photo-eyes hatched one after the other. the brain's roots dug deeper and deeper, entangling the earth and reaching into its depths till they knit into a boiling clew in the earth's nucleus. all this time, the faded moon shone frigidly at night on the empty shore and the improbable cerebral landscape.

iv. mechanical theatre

1.

Selen went out into the hall. Running his hand in the dark along the yielding walls so as not to get lost, he walked slowly in a circle, feeling for a way out. The tart smell of the full moon's ebb filled the air. Selen went outside and sat down on a step. The moon silvered his shin hair which overhung his slipping stocking. He groped for the lever and moved the moon closer so he could see it better. He poked the ground, its slack gray matter, with the toe of a shoe that another's wide foot had once worn. From the hollow that appeared a prehistoric face looked at him, a smooth gray skull. Selen wiped the dead brow clean of the moon's odorous secretions, which had filled the eye sockets and glistened there: glimpses of the moon. He weeded out from the hemispheres two or three young cherry trees, then tugged at the sagging lips and pulled them off the skull, along with the rest of the skin. The skin turned into a lump of dung in his hands. Selen kissed it on the lips.

Selen: So, smells like meat, doesn't it?

Lump of Dung: It's the violets. Nothing you can do about it in May.
Selen: I thought something was rotting. Look at the cracks in the floor. It can be anything, a corpse, say, or a rat.

The dung shook his doddering head sorrowfully.

3.

when I was my father, thought Selen, I killed this land killed it like a rat in a trap at that time it was alive with rain and life a stream throbbing in the rye it was total buggery he was my father this waste and I were like brothers in april the lilac spurts like spring pimples I was like a brother to my real father but my real brother was not a body his body was with him it was his property my brother was property I whispered this into his ear we were lying in spurred rye his ear was facing me white as flour with buttermilk mouldy like old milk and into this ear I tenderly whispered barely had time to jump away into the sea and clutch my head when he began growing over with crust rust I heard bolts spill out of him and sprockets leap I am telling you he was property father understood it but now he is sleeping I cannot imagine his dreams . . .

10.

Solon stands at the doorway. Selen approaches through the hallway, carrying Gertophia. Solon, greasy with lunar moisture (it oozes even out of his ears), wipes his hands hurriedly on Selen's hair and takes a few crumpled and faded photographs out of his pocket. Selen, surprised, lets Gertophia down and makes a long face. He holds in his wizened clinging hands an old shot of Gertophia with a broad smile and one naked, laden breast. A wrinkled little lizard face is resting in her palms. The nipple is large, brown, moist. The little face belongs to a head whose body has been cut off. The trachea and the vocal cords run up her wrists in an ivy of many snakes. The lunar fluid drenches Gertophia's hands and the infant's face. Wiping the photograph clean with the pad of his trembling finger, Selen stares and recognizes himself: the same agile skull; the same sweet liver held by fibers of tattered flesh; the same naked nervous system. It is from this breast that he used to drink snake and dandelion milk in the fields; a young Adonis and an ageing Venus. As though felled by a meteorite, Selen drops right on top of Gertophia's wizened body. He thinks that—once jammed into so tight a frame—incest becomes inevitable. The brain gives a soundless Homeric laugh, risking for the second time an awakening. Solon leaves his son alone with his doubts and rises as a pale apparition to the rapidly spinning, rustling moon which spills wet snowy confetti. Selen thoughtfully twists Gertophia's shoots on his finger and, whispering miching mallecho, the words everybody knows, falls his crying head onto her breast. With her last breath Gertophia, ripening and nearly edible, adjures Selen with God's carrot.

Anna Glazova lives in Chicago and Hamburg but writes in her native Russian. She has published two volumes of poetry, *Пусть и вода* (*Let Water*, Moscow, 2003) and *Петля. Невполовину* (*Loop. Unhalved*, Moscow, 2008). The present collection is a selection of her lyrical texts from over seven years.

Currently, Anna Glazova teaches Comparative Literature at Northwestern University (Evanston). In addition to her own writing, she has translated into Russian Robert Walser's *The Robber*, Ladislav Klima's *The Pilgrimage of a Blind Snake to the Truth*, and Unica Zürn's autobiographical prose.